ODE
TO
ANNA MOFFO
and
Other Poems

ODE
TO
ANNA MOFFO
and
Other Poems

□

Wayne
Koestenbaum

PERSEA BOOKS
New York

... works of imagination, not statements of fact. Names and incidents are either the product of the author's imagination, or are used fictitiously, and are not intended to reflect real persons or events.

The author gratefully acknowledges the editors of the following publications in which these poems first appeared:

The Agni Review: "The Answer Is in the Garden"
The Antioch Review: "Relics of the True Cross"
Boulevard: "The Ornate and Lovely Corner House," "A Professor Young and Old"
Epoch: "Tea Dance"
The Nation: "Fantasia on My Father's Gift"
Ontario Review: "Dog Bite"
The Paris Review: "A History of Private Life"
Shenandoah: "Doctor Type," "Fugitive Blue," "The Moving Occupations"
Western Humanities Review: "The Debut" (from "Ode to Anna Moffo")
The Yale Review: "Shéhérazade"

Under 35: The New Generation of American Poets, ed. Nicholas Christopher (Anchor/
    Doubleday): "The Moving Occupations," *"Shéhérazade"*
Poets for Life: Seventy-Six Poets Respond to AIDS, ed. Michael Klein (Crown): "The
    Answer Is in the Garden," "Doctor Type"

Library of Congress Cataloging-in-Publication Data

Koestenbaum, Wayne, 1958–
    Ode to Anna Moffo and other poems / Wayne Koestenbaum.
        p.   cm.
    ISBN 0-89255-154-2
    ISBN 0-89255-155-0 (pbk.)
    I. Title.
PS3561.0349O34   1990
811'.54—dc20   90-7641

Designed by Peter St. John Ginna
Set in Garamond by Keystrokes, Lenox, Massachusetts
Printed and bound by Haddon Craftsmen, Scranton, Pennsylvania
FIRST EDITION

For Steven Marchetti and Jeanne Schinto

CONTENTS

I

SHÉHÉRAZADE

1. *Asie*

One word, "nacreous,"
coils in me like a conch, a minaret,
or a question always in the process of being posed.
    My favorite part's *comme un*
immense oiseau de nuit, my bedtimes
moor in that glissando, even
      if I've planned a future
that gives love affairs
      no berth, a future stuck in its circuit like a sun. *Perse*

ou Chine are nice spots
on the map but don't try visiting them,
they will crumble in your fingers like a butterfly's wing.
    Even the felt fez
I bought at MGM's closeout sale
has an aura chalked on its brim:
    1940. I guess
some escapist flick
      wrung forehead-sweat from an extra, discoloring the rim.

    If I kiss the fez
I can almost taste his tribulation.
On my toilet lid sits a fragrant spirit, weak blue, called
    Eau de senteur à l'iris.
When I open it, out comes a djinn
named Shirley: she used to live in
    empty medicine vials
with *contrapposto*
      curve when turned upside down. Can you smell by hearing? *Asie*

smells like the floral
print my aunt wore to the fireworks the year
she died. But I imagine that she took a bargain junket
    and "went native," like Gauguin,
staying in the tropics with a woman
she loved. What I hear enters me,
    Ravel scored it so
the tremor in *voir*
    makes me clench my rectum. In *Chine* it dizzied me to sit

    by the chaperone's
plum pudding embonpoint: she should have been
minding her own daughter, a girl discovering the world
    in the hand of her flutist-
boyfriend unbuttoning her blouse—fjord
in a training bra. I know this
    from legend. That evening
in Shanghai, pleading
    nausea, she kept the audience waiting for a half hour

    and then never played—
her hands paralyzed as a consequence
of romance. Or had she swallowed poison? Strangely, the girl
    who hadn't played was received
favorably by the Shanghai press, who saw
her lack of "tone color" as one
    flaw in an otherwise
magical evening—
    drifting now away from me. When I cry *Asie, Asie,*

    my own breasts are just
visible below my arm's equator,
for I am Ingres' Odalisque, a jewel, like a spit globe,
    dropping from my ear but seized
by happiness at the latitude
where pain is supposed to begin,
    and staying there forever,
slave to a moment's
    dream that land is liquid, that there's no prime meridian.

2. La Flûte enchantée

A common complaint is that words are not kinetic.
An Egyptian fag
    dangles from the rouged lips
of Reynaldo Hahn—in Proust's bed—
humming "Si mes vers avaient des ailes."
    Nothing I can write will have
such wings. Is there a word in French like "fag"
for cigarettes, or only in the English of Dick Whittington?

    Reynaldo's hair is not more whitened now, there is no
deeper wistfulness
    it can achieve. The art
of sitting still I never learned,
I longed to be the Winged Victory
    seeming to fly but staying
fixed, as slender boys with artistic tastes
molt into husbands, shedding lisps. The dead grandfather

    I never met has a nicotined look in pictures,
as if he were steeped
    in smoke, a black cherry
compote in cordial handed down
for generations. No one eats it,
    but the seersaying sissy
curious about metamorphosis
questions this crystal ball in which a sodden cherry floats,

    he dredges the glass for secrets. To be torn apart
is my ambition,
    not, like Actaeon, limb
by limb, but in a prolonged waltz
of changes, every measure a new
    hiding-place opening up
within me, skin turning to bark, and back
to skin, as when the undressing dark camp counselor in

our cabin's ochre light turned to me as a painting
is caught by the glance
        of moonlight because the guard,
careless, has left the sash undrawn.
The flaw in primal scenes is that they
        happen, by definition,
only once. When mine happened, I was rapt
with the quest for ladybugs, my eyes on the ground to find

        coordinates of a world threatening to take wing.
My first song, "Frère
        Jacques," made me think our block
was bisected by a slender
ocean—not the song's words, but the song
        itself, the coin it carried
in its purse, convinced me there was a port
two houses down. But I found no harbor, no pirate ship—

        nothing but a front lawn lost in thought. Wouldn't you
run away to catch
        an ocean if it called
and asked for you by your first name—
as if the sea has plans for you, churning
        in memory of what you
do not know lies ahead, a future strange
as the fate of my friend Sue: riding to school, her new flute

        in the bike's basket, she made too sharp a turn and saw
her flute seem to fly
        willfully from its case
and land beneath a Mack truck's wheel!
Who could play a flute flattened by chance,
        its keys and air holes blended
so that she can't distinguish what is space
from what is silver, what is blank from what the wheel has filled?

3. L'Indifférent

Poor Daphne, changed into a laurel. Her lip—
    the lower one—is racked
by cold sores, always will be.
    Without such scars, how could I recognize
her nature? In a Venn diagram
she intersects the Daphne
    Industrial Park near the concert hall.
Why she is linked to an unleased lot, I cannot say,

nor why creepers grow in Eden to this day,
    an alphabet on rocks,
nor why, on a map, I share
    a bruise-colored crosshatched square with Ravel,
or my bandleader Mr. Tristan
overlaps with Yseult's Tristan.
    Praising me, he'd shout, "Good show!" I showed
and showed without pause to his—dare I say girlish?—face,

as if his bandroom were Tangier. He led us
    in a tango so tranced
it tore my life into parts
    like the eye those sisters bicker over—
never long in one socket before
they wrench it out. Poor eye, subject
    to the sisters' quarrels. That is why
antinomies sicken me, and why I prefer slow

students to quick ones: I loved the girl whose dream
    was winning a game show
from her living room's eyrie,
    her insights so piercing she needn't
appear in flesh as a contestant.
Angels carried her right answers
    to the TV studio, and coins,
as from a one-armed bandit, flooded her house. I, too,

am guilty of magic carpet rides. *Girlish*
  never refers to girls—
only to boys. It's a vast
  waste of breath to call a girl girlish, a boy
boyish. Why does the word "girlish" age
so inconspicuously, show
  so little tarnish, indifferent
to trends in usage, firm to its troubled course? The page

bleakly shimmers as the girlish boy decides,
  at last, to write his tale
of travel, having never
  crossed the border of his own creation,
the fence around his first disaster.
Twenty years ago, in the deep
  of my life, wondering if I could rise
to a bewilderment greater than age eight, I rode

my bike straight into a man who shouted, "Damn girl,
  watch out where you're going!"
He was drunk—so I reasoned—
  to mistake my sex. I enter the boy
I used to be, who lies in my bed,
naked, as if I've purchased him
  from an Arabian sorceress
who sews the body to its sorrow, invisibly.

FUGITIVE BLUE

My sister made up kennings for what she hated: "Socks Fall Down"
 Meant rolled-down socks with robin's-egg-blue patent leather
Mary Janes. I secretly loved fancy dress, but drowned
 My plumage in the closet where I hid my zither,
Xylophone and bells. I locked them in a box because I'd joined Cub Scouts
 And wished to kill the songbird, the prissy bluethroat

That I had been before I donned the regulation neckerchief.
 Fish gut veins and scouting knife were the same Prussian blue.
My merit badge for knots stood out from my navy shirt in bas-relief.
 Had they awarded a merit badge for fancy hairdos
I'd have won it, I took such pains to fix my Beatles bangs.
 But my attempt to be an outcast boomeranged,

For my mother, too, had a bowl-cut: coif of the novitiate.
 In a second box, I hid a trove of hats. Felt Robin Hood toque,
Vagrant's bowler, top hat, where are you now? Inanimate
 Beasts howled in a third box: a menagerie. The yoke
Of being father to so many stuffed animals weighed on my sleep
 Until I locked their urgent, speaking souls into the keep

Of the dark closet. But the boxes spread out force fields.
 Motley instruments and hats and animals were conscious
Of my pleasures in the world away from them. I swore fealty
 To these presences, but they knew I was promiscuous,
They knew I prayed to the party tray of nuts, to the bra
 Stained aqua when the laundry bled. Underwear was the ka,

The Egyptian immortal soul—postulated, rarely seen.
 I saw my ka resting like a bluejay on the windowsill
Beside the plastic troll I was to lose when with canteen
 I braved the woods. I gnawed its being to a standstill:
Chewed off the arms and head to find the inner troll,
 Then dropped the remnant in the dirt. I'd swallowed the soul,

What did I care for the body? But later I beseeched
    My father to drive back to the woods and rescue Troll.
The last I saw Him, he was mostly navel: but I preach
    The power of the severed part to sprout the whole.
I gazed straight into darkness when I discovered lint
    In my own navel: its smell was a doorway to a moment

I'd visited before. My second infernal discovery
    I made when dung-brown soiled the sleeve of my pajama top:
Corruptibility. Within my soul, I held an aviary:
    Cockatoos of a cobalt deep enough to blind rapped
Wings on my bars. I wanted to learn from the amorous
    Hippies how to be naked, how to wear violet shirts so luminous

I'd burn the retinas off my classmates. I saw the buttocks
    Of Ben Butler at Cub Scouts, and fancied his name was "Butter."
Or did I rename him because I felt elegiac,
    And knew the body's fate was to be eaten? In the gutter
We raced our paper sailboats to their desolation.
    Navigation was the mystery, not copulation:

Screwing I could conceive of, but not the watery course
    That I must sail. I tried my hand at hyperventilation;
I induced a faint. But the soul I tried to divorce
    From my body returned and rebuked me for the mutilation.
In seventh grade I bought a kerchief, with a clasp
    To anchor the silk's billowings: I prayed that like an asp

Its azure would sting me into the remoter country
    Where gypsies roamed, their caravans festooned along my scarf
Abstractly. I think I imagined the figures, as in palmistry
    One imagines lifelines, or as the larva
Predicts its sapphire wings. I wore this apache
    Scarf the first day of junior high: I thought I was Nijinsky,

Purely flame, celestial against the dowdy backdrop
    Of the multi-purpose room. But I'd misread the fashion trends:
No one was wearing apache scarves. I ate my meatball slop
    In solitude. The task was not to stand out, but to blend:
Thinking I was invisible, I wore the peacock
    Blue and found I was too visible. I wanted to shock

My public into cheers, until I learned that they were primitives,
    Thugs in leather, sluts in midriffs, bike chains
The only organza. Certain blues, like indigo, are fugitive:
    They fade. I never wore the apache scarf again.
Voyages ago I abandoned clothes that now I find, ultramarine
    Argosy in which the secret life is fully seen:

I remember now the clothes in which I lost my power.
    The ice blue Nehru shirt that zipped in the back
I wore to the party where I saw Ricky Sowers
    Feel up Carla. But Ricky, too, fought demons: his mother smacked
His face on Back-to-School Night. When Carla put her hand on Ricky's knee
    I saw my future's blueprint. I was wearing pants of lapis lazuli.

CASH

I waited to shave my faint mustache.
When Gary raised his hand in sixth grade, I peered
Beneath to see his first three scraggly hairs, and screamed
   "Attention, kids—Gary's got underarm hair!"
   I was a sentinel warning troops:
   "Underarm hair's invaded our shores. Prepare!"
When men don't shave, their faces at first turn green, like cash.
   I was prepared to turn green, and then to shave,
      But the green never came—and could I
   Shave a mustache weightless as dust on a leaf?
(Already I was so weary with maturity
      That I could neither move nor feel desire.)
      With Brad, I argued the pros and cons
   Of pubic hair, and bragged about my father:
"You've never seen such a halo of hair!" Brad quibbled,
   "Can you find his dick in that thicket?
      Chances are, his dick's invisible,
   Hidden like the Viet Cong in a jungle
Where our guns are useless. We must compromise between
   Hair mass and dick visibility, which stand
      In inverse proportion." Brad, the star
   Of Science Fair, knew hair, but he didn't bring
To the enterprise my passionate uncertainty—
   My sense that hair was the ghost, the second self
      Always around the corner, never
   To be faced, never to flash on me its smile
Of plenitude and endless coitus in hotel rooms
   We passed in the night on Highway 101.
      I waited to shave my faint mustache,
   But Brad said, "Why not shave it? Hair's the common
Currency of humanity. It'll grow back. Spunk,
   Too, will arrive under your pillow when you
      Least expect it. One morning you'll wake
   To find a peculiar gelatinous white
Foam from an unknown sea washed onto your hairless shore,
   And you won't even recall the sexy god

Who brought you love in a dream's covert."
But I could neither move nor feel desire.
When men don't shave, their faces at first turn green, like cash.
Was it the green of verdure, or of nausea?
Prescient Brad knew that for years I'd have
Dry orgasms, the sea heaving without spray.
Seek and ye shall find did not apply to my father's
Pubic hair: I searched to destroy but couldn't
Unveil him, plump pee-shy Salome
With blue boxers and just a Ken-doll blank plane,
I feared, where a penis should be. Semaphore of hair
On his arms signaled inscrutably: Shave. Shave.
I waited to shave my faint mustache.
Manhood, like the stock market, rises and falls—
When men don't shave, their faces at first turn green, like cash—
And in my childhood it crashed. Though funds dry up,
The dread of shaving stays damp. I thought
Of body hair as a Science Fair project—
I was the control, my classmates were the variables,
And the locker room was my laboratory.
Hair was an investment I feared
Might be fatal: did I dare plunge into hair?
I devised a *trompe l'oeil* way of being a girl: I tucked
My prick between my legs. It left a dimple.
I waited to shave my faint mustache
Until, lost in a damp grotto, I stumbled
Toward the medicine chest: the light fleece fell from my face
Like pale italics. My face would not be green
Like my father's face when he went days
Without shaving. What is it men do? They shave.
When men don't shave, their faces at first turn green, like cash.

EST-CE QUE

> *They lived on that road, drifting along its length
> here and there, according to the inexplicable im-
> pulses of their monstrous darkness.*
> —Joseph Conrad, "The Idiots"

I've graduated from Rossini's *Cinderella*
    In summer opera—*La Cenerentola*—
But teenage sex is still before me, school I never
    Matriculated at. My student with speech
Deficiencies and strong arms tempts me into scandal:
    What separates me from a professional
Pedagogue is that I admit to my dry colleagues
    Which students I'd be happiest molesting.
Tonight's opera is *Lucia di Lammermoor,* so
    I dovetail "The Idiots" class discussion
With confessions about my sometime raving sister—
    How each family bears its print of monstrous
Darkness. The music's stopped at the senior prom I missed:
    I make out nothing. A scrap of old gossip
That gives me a *frisson* of neurasthenic spine-shivers
    When I am not paying attention during sex
Is the story of Rick's long night on a car's back seat—
    One prom couple fornicating in the front,
Rick and his date in the back. Did each listen to each?
    I still consider that scene the pinnacle
Of teenage potential, and my Liszt étude practice
    Beneath my parents' demented Van Gogh print
At sweltering noon as that age's shameful nadir.
    No sound is capable of resonating
Like arms I never caressed on make-out movie-dates.
    I could spend the rest of my creative life
Listing, with a penitent's urgency, the gym boys
    I have furtively studied. Child who adored
All species of the undressed, I compiled "Nudism
    Handbooks," construction-paper-bound biweeklies:
Volume III, hid in the jacket of a Schnabel disk
    Containing "Invitation to a Waltz"—too

Warped to play, his record's melted greatness camouflaged
    My smut—featured my cursive copy of *Time*'s
"I am Curious (Yellow)" piece; a reduced Titian
    Venus; *Reader's Digest* on the scourge of porn;
Vanessa Redgrave's arms crossed over breasts in *Blow Up*
    (Clipped from *Ramparts*); editorial I penned
On *Adam*'s superiority to magazines
    Like *Cavalier* that did not picture each sex
Frontally. Dionysian, inclusive, a tyke
    Walt Whitman, how could I foresee the iron
Curtain of seventh grade darkening the horizon—
    Hour of "Dress and Run," "Slaughter Ball," mnemonic
Devices that help me recall that reign of terror?
    On cold days, ballroom dancing replaced football.
My partner Sheila, who lunched on her Thermos of soup
    Instead of the snack-bar Sloppy Joes and subs
Hard boys craved, bragged that she was weaving tap-dance routines
    Into our awkward waltz: Sheila, devotee
Of *Naughty Marietta,* the popular slut's twist
    Made your tap steps look prissy. Now for school lunch
I'm brave, I bring your girlish egg salad. Mystery
    Deeper than Golgotha: one morning I woke
Sadly estranged from the opposite sex. Opposite?
    I used to time my party appearances
With the believer I dated, so we could make out
    In the public eye, long soupy French kisses
Directed at my friends' envious peeping. I leave out
    Her wronged name. My life is illuminated
By one sin so engulfing, the domino years cave
    In around it—a kind of thought I save for
Limbo moments: dozing in a car, or vacuuming.
    I may be scrubbing my linoleum floor
When the memory of the high school dance I did not
    Care to feel her body at—or the dances
Unattended (teenage boys wear habits, too, take vows)—
    Warns me that Rick's back-seat motion is a force
Still ranging. Sheila monopolized three periods
    Giving her oral report on *The Good Earth,*
The plot's every inch displayed. Her full retelling seemed
    One prolonged washing of the hands to rinse off

Every stain of the plot, so we might hold the infant
     Fable's kernel, and admire. I chose *Jane Eyre*
For my report, though the teacher said *Northwest Passage*
     Was the more boyish book. I seek no passage.
I watch these reruns as if they were fresh news. I read
     The books I desire, under lightbulbs I burn.
My favorite French construction was always *est-ce que.*
     Is it that I am hungry? *Is it that I*
Hear the wreck of a car? When my brother began French
     Two years before me, I envied his *bonheur;*
Learning makeshift French myself from an imperfect book,
     I stumbled on the pronunciation of
Est-ce que. Even after years of French I am not
     Legally bilingual. *Is it that* I yearn
To speak two things at once? *Est-ce que je brûle de dire*
     Deux choses en même temps? My brother learned the tongue
I coveted; I struggled with *est-ce que*'s logic
     While seatbelted in our lemon Rambler's
Back seat, and made out French's vague outline. Boy and girl
     Face each to each in the dance's separate lines
And meet to waltz in the circle the two regimes share.
     My students don't understand the power of
Multiple point-of-view, nor do they see how we are
     All idiots, not merely those born thinking
Slowly. One student says the mentally-ill receive
     Too much attention; she doesn't drop spare change
In rattling cups. Is it that I am familiar with
     My monstrous darkness, that I think of handing bums
Dollar bills, but never do? Is it that when Sheila
     Sits down after her long report, she has made
The bad earth good? Thank God the City Opera uses
     Supertitles, so I can read the English
When Cinderella forgives her cruel stepsisters in
     Italian, draws with her voice a commonwealth
In which everything I burn to say at once resides.

TEA DANCE

"Young men always expose themselves to me on Amtrak.
    Am I so plain that they think I can't refuse?
Fire Island is a shadow of its former self.
    The days I miss, when men jacked off on stoops
Along Christopher Street: I didn't have to get dressed
    Or leave my building to find a trick." Thus spake
My hairdresser. After I dreamt that Darjeeling tea
    Was synonymous with genius, I tasted
The word *tea* for days, mystified. Then I remembered
    Tea dances: the dance I stared at a swarthy
Mesopotamian stele of a man and felt
    His member in the bathroom. These are the fleet
Radiances I return to when I swim in the lane
    Made tempestuous by the thrashing freestyle
Of a man whose laps I time with mine so that we meet,
    As if by accident, at the side, and stare
At each other through blue goggles. Will I behold him
    Languidly soaping his ass in the shower
As if I'm not watching? I always watch. I don't wrap
    My towel around my loins, but parade between
Sink and toilet with abandon: the stalls have no doors,
    So I observe in the mirror, while combing
My hair, a Professor Emeritus. How I love
    The sight of genius striving to defecate!
In the Japanese tea ceremony, the seating
    Mirrors the cosmos: my tea ceremony
Takes place in memory—my mother's Constant Comment,
    My silent father shunning tea for Sanka.
Threat of hysterectomy hung over my childhood
    Like a cloud of locusts—wasn't my mother
Always on the verge of one? Why does sapless mint tea
    Bring me back to my father's vasectomy?
Am I morbid to return in imagination
    To the place where I began—the ligaments
And chambers of my father's reproducing genius,
    His genitals a kind of feudal guild hall,

Good pewter on the table? On Boston's underground—
    The T—a young man who asked me for the time
Pressed his leg against mine between Government Center
    And Copley stations—a recuperative
Idyll. Like a shady priest, or mesmerist, he drew
    A holiness from me, without saying his name.
Krafft-Ebing grotesques are now my domesticities,
    What I see in the mirror. My hairdresser:
"In the smoking car, a cute boy—scandalously young,
    Maybe thirteen—played footsie with me, and when
Lights flickered and went out at New Haven, he flashed me
    And played with himself. I tried to look kindly.
I didn't want to discourage his professional
    Ambitions, so early in the boy's career."
As a boy, I stayed after school to discuss revolt
    In the colonies—the Boston Tea Party—
With my history teacher: I hoped he'd seduce me.
    I wore jeans that rode low, a shirt that rode high,
To trick him into forgetting morals. But I lived
    By the light of this theology: the hands
That caress Mozart's limpid phrases cannot also
    Touch cock. Did my father—shy in his boxers,
His urinating a remote rill in a far room
    I was barred from—encourage this chaste belief?
Do I think that the tea leaves would have told differently
    If my father had invited me to watch
His toilette, if he had taken me into his bath?
    I once vowed that if I grew into a full
Adult male I would spend my days before a mirror
    Marveling that I had passed over Jordan,
And had not been left, a eunuch, on the other shore.
    My body has become the body I thought
Was a distant, desired star, but this has brought no change.
    My best friend from high school is still my best friend:
Then, our favorite joke was the man in Emergency
    With a carrot broken off in his rectum.
It's been years since I saw my friend nude in the boys' gym
    We now admit to each other was a place
In which we willed our members down by thinking of death.
    How much more gripping our lunches might have been

If, over bologna, I had said to my soul's twin:
    "Did you notice that Coach Wasserman's penis
Seems waterlogged, inhumanly long, like a dildo
    Or the kind of apparatus a sex-change
Patient dreams of acquiring? Did you notice how red
    And juvenile Craig's prick looks? Like a crayon
With its paper wrapper, a foreskin, worried away.
    And Robert's is like a cougar's lolling tongue!
He beat off in his clubhouse to the tune of his dad's
    Jazz singles and porno playing cards that showed
Cotton candy pubic hair." I gave my best friend bites
    Of my sandwich every day: my mother piled
Meat generously, his mother gave only one slice.
    Would it have ruined the universe's plans
If we had touched each other, or discussed at leisure
    The parts of friends, or if I'd said: "My father's
Is not so enormous. I am not frightened by it.
    It has the guilelessness of the animals
God loves the best. What is your father's like? Will you grow
    To match it? It's nice having something to live
In anticipation of, like a cadence that haunts
    The first movement, though it happens in the third.
If we were to touch, what would be our first position?
    I certainly couldn't put yours in my mouth
Unless you washed it first. And what about geometry,
    The proofs we were assigned? I'll prove that the point
Of prayer is exactly this, though your youth group leader
    Would disagree: this longing is the reason
Ancient Greece is justly famous, and why the vases
    Possessed me in the museum—not the jade
We were required to study, but the huge erections
    Of the gods—oddly uninviting, like spears,
Or the toothpicks with which one seizes cocktail hotdogs.
    Brave Bull—the bowling alley—might be a good
First place to try: brave men have drilled peepholes in the walls
    Between toilet stalls, and if you're shy you can
Watch the kaleidoscopic panorama of men
    Passing your window, even if you don't
Scrawl your intentions on a square of toilet paper
    With a Bic pen and pass it to your partner—

Like square dancing, or bridge, a ritual you can learn.
    I love being hypnotized. Am I a good seer?
I am trying to be a clear medium through which you
    Can hear the past speaking as it wished to speak.
May the trance never end. This is how I feel when tea,
    Mystical Darjeeling, rinses out my sight
So I can see the heartache in the center. Is this
    Truly the past? It's not as dark as you said—
Not as gloomy. Are you sure I'm not in the present?
    Look down at my body to reckon if time
Has altered it. Did you see Kevin's penis standing
    At half-mast? What turned him on? The wrestling match?
I think I will grow up to be an expert on flesh,
    I gaze at it so. My penis has blossomed
To the size of a small doughnut because I played it
    For too many thrills last night, watching Popeye
When my parents were gone. It's not that I thought Popeye
    Was erotic, but I had to watch something,
I had to fill my mind with images. Images
    That plague me now will turn to paradise
In twenty years. I must have patience. The stalking men
    Will rise from comic strips, like dead from their graves,
And plant my mouth with kisses. I am not alone here:
    Listen to the water. This is a trance,
But when I wake I will know everything that has passed,
    And what I am dreaming now I will turn
Into daily life—and though in this childhood I can't
    Talk out of turn, I will never stop talking
In that future where it is eternally my turn."

A HISTORY OF PRIVATE LIFE

First came the age of gold, then silver, steel,
papier-mâché—and now glass: the transparent

    briefcase I bought in Rome so you can see
    the secret contents (book, pen, fruit) I lug

up opaque streets. These are not privacies.
One street abuts another; reticence

    confirms them as hushed individuals.
    My neighbor pronounces "opaque" *o-pack*.

As in: "Oh, pack your bags and go!" His wife,
Greek, wears tight jeans that suggest the imprint,

    the fossil-mark, of her privacy. I shield
    my eyes, not wishing rudely to behold

her "v," though she has placed it on display.
My house sits next to the "o-pack" man's own:

    books huddled on his refrigerator,
    as if history needed keeping cold.

The four swans afloat (sharing a private
joke) on Hadrian's Villa's pond do not

    protect or protract mourning. They are true.
    Friends fresh from a Bombay ashram fed them seed.

Less true are palace fronts no longer whole.
Sky space between cracked pillars assembles

    a tremulous, flesh-coral sense of night.
    The stone of any saint's basilica,

beheld through dreaming eyes, becomes the man's
cracked ribcage fossilized so I can run

    a curious thumb along his frame and pluck
    bone souvenirs—as if martyrdom weren't

indigenous to the one who suffers,
but a scent or quality one can steal.

    I lean on irony to see. Five men
    spent August painting my house (front and back)

yolk-yellow. Gentle private men, they slashed
my tree's branch because it leaned on the house

    and stood in their way. I watched the slashing
    silently. A racing panic forbids

completion of this line: the painters stare
in as I type these words . . . Spenser's Una

    peered into the glass and saw another
    rhyme's thorns prick her. She knew it was August

thirty-first, as blossoms out my window
tremble with opinions, advice from wind,

    horn-blasts, late loud parties—these ambient
    disturbances the tree absorbs through sap

while living out its pageant of cell loss
and gain, its didactic dead leaf carpet

    telling the children (this or any year)
    who gather beneath, that they will recall

this leaden sky as argent. I do not
own land but am landlord of a sadness,

not sculpted like the trim *jardin anglais*
peering down from the tag sale print I've placed,

tilted, above a mirror, so staring
at myself I peripherally see

gardens dragged by gravity, though I trust
mechanical laws keep pictures in their frames,

against the walls they were meant to uphold.
It's not a pure pleasure to be French-kissed—

sometimes the lover's tongue assaults the mouth's
sense of tabernacle, though a rushing

anticipation—immanence like skirts—
makes the locked jaw lax and willing. Autumn

demands to exist (we comply): mythic
events occur in time not wrenched by watch

but in a hazed forgetfulness, as when
I use a stolen guest towel to dry

my body and detect no scent of theft,
or Warsaw appears through nocturnal mist

as home to the man (hewn glance!) I pursue
down love-cobbled alleys, meanwhile thinking

"Communist life is not as bad as one
has heard." Quest, knight, lady, beast: these lies make

up anatomy. One struggles to paint
railings, pediments, and September comes

with my house's bulk looming unpainted
against mute neighbor homes, with aged or young

residents—or no residents at all.
Some boats, bound by rope, rest against the dock,

    and others float in lichen's privacy,
    though I'm not sure what privacy means:

a tremor, it starts when the painters leave,
then spreads up the spine, bringing glimpses

    of September twenty-third and its slant
    velvety relation to the ideal.

My house, unpainted, becomes archaic,
for the average American bedroom

    (middle-class) contains a microcosm
    of a French eighteenth-century pleasure

palace complete with folly, vista, pond,
and the possibility of drowning.

FANTASIA ON MY FATHER'S GIFT

For safe mailing, he sealed the box with too much
tear-proof tape—as if with stays or feeding tubes

　　its body, heavy, celestial, clumsy,
　　had been cinched. Think of the word *lourde,* containing

healing (Lourdes) and homely *(laid)* and getting laid.
I cowered before the task of cracking it.

　　I treated the scissors like an X-acto
　　knife, foreswearing the holes where in crab fashion

first finger and thumb cooperate to cut.
I did not scissor conventionally; I

　　knived, though these are classical sewing scissors
　　stolen from my mother, who barely figures

in this story. The box was honestly white,
though the tape had yellowed on its postal trip.

　　My scissor's blade thrust between the twin box-flaps,
　　a valley or canal where tape must perform

its own resistance, but some of the wire-backed
crosshatchings pointed left and others pointed

　　right, so no single gesture could thwart them all.
　　I had to find the tape's beginning and break

its continuity, slit a vein and peel
back the spiraling strips as in a '50s

　　mummy film at Fox Theatre where the lobby
　　tried to be a labyrinth and succeeded:

in the box, forced open, I saw the same
Styrofoam pellets my cautious father stuffed

    among my record player's parts to prevent
    its mind from ruin during shipping thirteen

years ago (it arrived ruined): now I found,
on the Styrofoam bed, two moonrocks swaddled

    shut in taped plastic, each unclassified weight
    synesthetically reminiscent of sounds

at Point Lobos where seals choraled (my father
found them musical, he was wearing a coat

    whose plaid I should filially reproduce
    as if poems were pacts and not indiscretions

murmured to keep oneself alive): and within
the tape lay a deeper plastic, reinforced

    with eyeball-shaped air pockets that childish hands
    love to pop: within this glaucous diaphragm

asking politely to be punctured I found
a cloth the color of the solar system

    or the velvet lap on which engagement rings
    and the less serious friendship rings are laid

for safekeeping, seduction, and emphasis
in a jeweler's window: this violinist's

    chamois contained two lumps starting to attain
    a nominal absoluteness in my hand:

I spoiled the fabric by scissoring it up
and found, inside, a smeary newsprint photo

of two male dignitaries shaking hands while
a woman in a checked dress (interpreter?)

looked on: nested in the newspaper, some white
crepe paper which I poked through, uncovering

two candles, though the word "candle" came to me
after puzzling. Here is what I saw, and see.

They are heart-sized, a cow's heart, not a chicken's;
not faceted, but bordering the country

of facets; unsure of their shape; arctic, clumped.
They lie in limbo between glass and crystal,

though isn't crystal just a duchy of glass?
These opaque objects flirt with transparency

and through their mottled amorphous sides I see
the white wax interior, the mystery,

the candle itself, which I must separate
semantically from the candleholder: one

is squat and perfumed and has a tendency
to melt, the other's molecules refuse,

by birthright, to have intercourse with ash.
The crystal fits its candle as a holster

hugs its pistol. My father mailed these ice-rocks
from Detroit, city of riot, with no note;

the gift speaks for itself. Packed circumspectly,
the candles and their cages reached me entire.

I light the wicks: one catches, the other fails
to strike up an acquaintanceship with fire,

for this shy thread is imbedded in tallow
and only shows, above the ground, a fraction

of flesh, as though it were maladroit at sports
and could not rise to the occasion of air.

EROTIC AND SEPULCHRAL EPIGRAMS
FROM THE CINQUECENTO

I.

The same example applies to the excoriated
and the adored-by-God,
the single and the betrothed,
each sighing in his own time.

My "liege," my "love,"
I heard your Venetian accent
as (forgive me!) a refusal to turn,
a walking tempo, a lassitude.

I was wrong. Virtue's semblance adorns
the most lenient and fiery women in their twenties.
Of course, you, lamenting,
heard novenas said for Mother in the old town

where night seems, as in Giotto,
a quiescence, an aspiration,
like thinking alone with a pressing doubt
reminding me what it is to be an "I" living

as a "Mr." or "*Signore*," seen nimbly
extricating himself from the table,
painfully moving from dinner to dinner
to a virtuous destination, miles distant.

2.

. . . with averted
eyes, young indicated women like us

sotto voce but with temerity beg
Giovan Battista (you who can't
escape from poverty)
to strike us across the neck and remind us of sensation.

It's been a long time since I've said my vespers.
　　Chiaroscuro of
earth sometimes united with itself and sometimes riven . . .

3.

Here's dawn undressing like a minor seventh.
　　I want to fly, Lord, then I don't want to fly:
for contraries I have a modern heart.

　　Ecstasy is viral. I caught it, staying out late.

When I mature, I will go with Flavio
　　to the place where men meet their negatives.

4.

Dear God, what adventures I had in Rome!
　　Yes, for no *lire,*
but for silver's point, its way

of conducting tension
　　to the bone
(charity befell me because I kissed God)
　　you admitted having sojourned at Pietro Bembo's

and begged my pardon in the Colosseum
　　(charity befell me because I kissed God).

I dived into myself, after Eleanor and her sister
　　used me as an illustration of ungainliness.

5.

Felice is happy, a million times over:
　　made amorous by a real man's sport.
In the hotel, she remembered
　　elations of previous years,

when, though poor and suspicious,
    certain cruelties of the abyss
might be said to have *wept* their way
    into her method of seeing the universe

as papal and vile at once.
    Despite her fragile egoistic hunches,
a coarse Alpine
    air made love to the river in her—

a daughter mincing, conscientiously.

6.

O God,
    you who told me so, that last time,
when you pressed your potency against my
    will to possess, my "I" . . .

I pass the hours
    in a torched landscape bereft of parallels.

7.

I laughed through my nostrils the long ride home,
    passing Pitti Palace, the House of Life—

we laughed at my wife,
    hoping for her wealth—
O who didn't laugh at the costermongers
    among us cadging dimes?

Meanwhile the year coursed past us in its silk . . .

Sins, pardoned before committed,
    ask to be repeated, as a knife
begs to be seen as timid and mollified.

Neither time nor fortune counts as condition.
　　Only the soul—"death," in common parlance—
is dry enough to arouse suspicion.

Donna, you made error after error
　　spiritually and thus I'm dolorous.
You pleased me less and less each spring
　　on account of your bony infinity.

As always I was indiscreet.
　　Such as: when spiritually unquiet
I sensed dinner arriving and dried my tears
　　and screamed *everything is love in this sodden world.*

Nobody understood my distress:
　　fish renascent from the Book of Esther,
color of talons, of hibiscus,
　　Donna, your chignon, your suspiring,

colt leaping over fences and never falling
　　and never betraying its name,
lady of the borderless old world's misery,
　　Donna, fresh cold blade of the castrato's axe!

9.

Most armies, when Love knocks, rush to the door,
　　but Giovanni, honorable new-found friend,
I find you pitiless, without end.
　　May no rumor obscure the song
of your exit, which wine bursting from its jug

could not rival in repleteness and a slight tinniness.
　　You sway me: slave in the house of Oh My.
I've gone two steps toward ardency
　　without doubting
the sensations that nightly crowd my spine.

10.

This is how I consider flowers: they cascade,
    they complain, a divisive

way of glimpsing gold
    in every vivid, pessimistic thing:
including Venus, or the fiendish
    interpretation we give ellipses,

when blankness means us no harm.

II

ODE TO ANNA MOFFO

I. The Debut

I.

What possesses me,
a maenad, is her first entrance,
when only the boy reading the liner notes
    absolutely knows
it is Anna Moffo and not
an impostor about to open her mouth
    and derange the air
    with a tone
introspective as a plant
alone with thoughts of her stem and her photosynthesis.

On loose-leaf paper
I wrote down the names of the stars.
My roster still sleeps in the *Butterfly* case,
    as if *dramatis*
personae were frozen there
like Easter Island idols, punished, alert,
    exiled in a box
    whose fragrance,
when I open it, is dust
mingled with narcissus, scent of what I will never have:

    presence of her voice
    in the house
alive, so I may applaud,
while wind from a special effects machine streams through her hair.

2.

An ode's a body
on the witness stand, under oath
to explain itself. I played the piano
    with forcep fingers;
I watched the first knuckle for flaws—
spots where the devil might gain admittance.
    I pared my diet
    to be clear
of debt: I wanted to owe
nothing to the world, and dreaded the sound of translucent

    human horn clicking
against insensate ivory.
Embarrassed by my nails, archaic armor,
    I cut them so short
that to endure a simple fugue
I had to cover the sore, pink tips with gauze.
    Tenderly I plunged
    to the C
major resolution, shocked
that the bass and soprano lines should finally concur,

    while, in the next room,
    my mother
stirred meat into the evening
sauce—its simmering music muted by a sliding door.

3.

My arpeggios
were seasick representatives
of dead men's wishes. *Robert's Rules of Order*
    controlled the affairs
of parliaments, but not of hands
whose phrases, madeira, had high alcohol
    content that burned off
    in my sleep:
Bach's B-flat Partita woke
remembering, through a hangover's vapors, my attempt

to break, in nineteenth-
century style, its prelude's chords,
dispersing what should be single. English Suites
    are made of distinct
dances—gigues, courantes, allemandes—
cooperating to compose an empire.
    I played with cold touch
    so the lines
could voice their separate demands.
Découpage is sentimental. But I use it to keep

    memories in place;
    through clear paste
I remember sarabandes,
stiff, costumed, lit by a naked light bulb's Ursa Minor.

4.

    Beginner's pieces—
parlor offerings by Kuhlau,
Hummel, Beethoven—hide unsuspected depths,
    though without pedal
it is hard to blur the sudden
harmonic changes and make them sound prolonged.
    I played Clementi
    while seated
on a violet pillow
beside my demonstrating teacher; I rubbed my finger,

    on the velour, back
and forth, for Japanese garden
effects, creating and then erasing waves,
    as the sea crashes
and recedes in a pebbled yard
whose garden hose is far from water. The will
    of the teacher, hand
    beating time,
helps phrases find their shadows
on the adjacent page. The sonatina was a tide

too full of seaweed,
    jellyfish,
and the unexplained, to ask
my body to wade more deeply than a knee's trembling height.

                        5.

    Trio sonatas,
duets, and quartets: they appall.
I played the "Spring" Sonata, or its likeness,
        on a Yamaha
whose keys were wax museum men—
parricides—caught in the acts that brought them fame.
        The violinist
        scraped and sawed.
My left hand was distracted
by a vision of the solitary hair, like a taut

        bow's gut string, that grew
unfettered from the breast I'd touched,
with an accompanist's awe, the night before.
        I changed a quartet's
first chord: with a single error,
I turned A major to A minor, and slept
        beside pats of dung
        and the cows'
swaying matutinal flesh
as the sun rose in Santa Cruz above the fenced-off field

        where my date and I
        smelled of hay
transformed by crime into gold;
we'd spent the night together, though in separate sleeping bags;

6.

she had learned to play
cello overnight, undoing
diligent years at the violin. We switch
    instruments to soothe
the blister of consistency.
My lips buzzed from "The Carnival of Venice";
    I couldn't evoke
    gondolas
with my faulty embouchure,
nor could I reproduce the breast in Giorgione's "Tempest."

Double and triple
tonguing ("tu-ku" and "tu-tu-ku") bestowed
a useless velocity. Where could I go?
    Mired in low culture,
I was aching to reach the high,
but hardly knew that Arban's medicinal,
    plodding manual
    on trumpet
technique stored jewels from *Norma,*
or that sounds from my brass bell had consanguinity

with a woman's voice,
    soprano
cornet blurting its salute
while water, discontented, gurgled behind the spit valve.

7.

My teacher's father,
hacking into a handkerchief,
took his constitutional by the living
    room's two concert grands,
while, against the punctuation
of sputum, his spinster daughter heard my scales.
    Another teacher
    bravely limped
on stage to bow with one hip
higher than the other: steel parts implanted at the waist

kept her in motion.
Debussy's "Arabesques" succored
the woman who wore a neck brace and took shots
    once a month to bring
movement back, for a ghostly hour,
to stiffened hands. I entered the studio
    during one private
    Faustian
flourish, her fingers fiery
beneath the framed, clinical, admonitory photo

    of a master's hands—
    some prewar
Titan. "Excuse me," she said,
and put away her Debussy to teach me counterpoint.

8.

My trumpet teacher
died from overplaying the tape
of his solo, long ago, in some Passion—
    "the gem of the coast,"
he called the seaside festival
in which his solo curled like a common green
    within a finer
    malachite.
We listened to his triumph
beside a lidless upright converted to an ashtray.

    He slicked his hair back
with an odorless oil, and scalp
glimmered within the grooves left by the comb's teeth.
    He rented the shack—
a tool shed crossed by trumpetweeds—
to a mystery man, more hypothesis
    than man, who never
    showed his face,
but must have heard the one Bach tape
pealing amidst the passacaglia of Scotch bottles

crashing in garbage
cans left out
in the immaculate town
of Los Gatos, stucco houses buried among vineyards.

9.

My debut is dark—
a kindergarten cameo
appearance playing imported tambourine.
    I stood on the stage
and rattled a white disk, waiting
for the curtain to drape my futility.
    Reward for ceaseless
    and timely
performance was candy corn.
I bit the black stripe off the triangle and saved the heart

    of the confection—
an orange, blunt pyramid—for a day
when I could comprehend its antecedents.
    We learned to read notes
by a perverse pedagogy;
semibreves hovered outside the pale of clef
    or staff, and we guessed
    pitch by faith,
deprived of system. I gripped,
with the will of a colonialist, my tambourine,

    as if it were sky
    stirred, jangled,
and abandoned by a boy's hand,
as if the sky depended on a boy to make it sound.

10.

I craved a *succès*
d'estime in *The Wizard of Oz;*
my role—Farmer Munchkin—had twenty-four lines,
    each a trim bonsai
truncated by the script's design.
After the house fell on the witch, in Act One,
    my task was to make
    a florid
pass at Dorothy, while she,
in a cantor's grieving tremolo, regretted Kansas.

    Instead, I adored
the shy rehearsal pianist
whose sideburns intimated future movements,
    son of a busty
dwarf who drank and drove and taught him
rudiments of musicianship: voice-leading,
    transposition, touch,
    and closure.
I longed to enroll at her
hard school—to be flayed alive, like Marsyas, for singing.

    She took no pupils.
    I spent nights
learning kabalah, counting
my sheet's seams—a numerology war against myself.

11.

    Of Esther's perfumed
indifference to the enemy
our chorus sang at the Purim carnival,
    though no one listened;
I aimed my song's bow-and-arrow
at an old woman wandering through the crowd.
    She was, I supposed,
    my first grade
teacher spending holidays
in search of former pupils; she scoured the news for clues

of our whereabouts
so she might shock some renegade
in his tracks and tell him that she'd long foreseen
    the predicament
puzzling him now. But this woman—
when I approached her—was a stranger, a song
    without words, who stared
    at my face
as if recognizing it,
and then vanished into the carnival's obscurity.

    In a moment's space
    a strong wind
has entered my room and blown
about my Moffo articles, which I left neatly piled

                    12.

    on my desk's center;
now, the gust-scattered clippings fan
out from an imagined nucleus like fronds
    of a child's pinwheel,
or like a tropic flower stretched
on the rack of the seasons it has suffered.
    I think that Anna
    Moffo sings,
to this day, in a second,
parallel Met, a hologram of the original

    projected in air,
where failing voices continue
to thrive amidst a system of strange geysers
    and girders, cables
linking the golden prompter's box
to a sky that burns directly on the stage.
    She made her debut
    at the Met
on Saturday, November
14, 1959, a matinee repeated

the moment I mail
    this letter,
addressed to Miss Moffo, care
of the mind's Met, where Broadway joins forgotten avenues.

II. The Letter

1.

Anna, I've waited ten years for this hour:
it's time to sketch your love of arriving late
to the beat, your wet attack's impalpable power.
A tattered *Who's Who* taught me that your fate
was vocal breakdown: no records compensate
(not even Gold Seal's *Traviata,* reissued
at a slashed price) for seeing you hesitate
on the old Met stage brink, for hearing you
appear in your prime, or give a broadcast interview.

2.

You wore your voice down with unwise Lucias.
You, alone, should have picked which parts to sing.
Pushy men! (I'm male, but only loosely.)
On the Canteloube cover, your silk dress clings
to the flesh in floral folds, a fist crumpling
categories. You hum, close-mouthed, of rain
in Villa-Lobos. His music suits your crooning:
you can't sing solids. Life began to stain
your voice in '66; that date's the carrion my brain,

3.

a vulture, circles—crossroads where the air
in your throat consumed the adamant. Your sound
decayed; no desperate lessons could repair
(however fine a coach) the damage done.
I hear it first in the Gluck set, where you're thin,
miscast Euridice, against Verrett.
Was Gluck prescribed as purgative? Plutonium,
but stored, glacé, is how I'd describe your Met
debut, though I must wait millenia to buy a ticket

4.

for November '59, when your "Amami, Alfredo!"
moved cognoscenti. I heard you once, live, late:
you sang "Tacea la notte," hair coiled, alfresco
in Baltimore's Melody Tent, tugboat lights
and popcorn smell clotting the wharf-soft night.
Before your entrance, I saw you adjust the chopstick
in your bun for a *South Pacific* look, pulled tight.
That was '81. Your trills, oil slicks,
mercilessly miked, showed rich ore in the derrick

5.

of your body, upright, regal against the acoustic
shield that bounced sounds back to us. I taped
the program to my wall—too well. It stuck.
When I tried to scratch it off, your photo, cropped
flatteringly, stayed, as if a lens had stopped
looking, or learned to balance on the brink
of sight, and never fall. Meek, I chopped
necessaries below your picture, linked
forever to my kitchen wall. One critic said the "stink"

6.

of your *Thaïs* rose from the gaudy ad-campaign's
"Incomparable Moffo." He wrote, "Her high C
suggests the spectrum." No voice is venison—
lasting, salted. I'll make chronology
blindingly clear: when you sang "Un bel dì"
at your Rome debut, sweetheart, I wasn't born;
I was zero when you blazed as TV's Butterfly,
hosted "The Anna Moffo Show," and penned
a hit pop song, "Città"; nor could I *bis* you in Milan—

7.

martinet Karajan's note-floating Nannetta.
I hunt through sale bins to see what's still
alive of your legacy—an operetta
CD, "A Song for You." For me? You spill
from bar to bar, but your Lehár's never shrill.
Those tracks, from '62, lay half-produced
in dark, expectant studio vaults until
you authorized release. Did you excuse
the session's flaws, afraid that otherwise we'd lose

8.

a jeweled document? You bragged of boas
in *Life,* and lungs strong as a gladiator's.
"Miss Pin-Up," beamed *Corriere della Sera.*
"Anna Moffo, as a name," you said, "like Greta
Garbo, is euphonious, from a bygone era."
As a young girl, you longed to be a nun.
I keep your clippings, xeroxed, arranged by year,
in a black filebox; within my circle, not one
friend knows I love these smudged tokens of your fortune.

9.

Anna, your eyes are escalator steps
gliding toward the mezzanine's fancy shops;
each iris gleams below a fan of lashes, and spins off
from its mate; your moon-wide orbs regard
the camera from unconnected oblique angles;
your eyes are Tinder Box saucers, a *ritard*
taken to heart, so languor grows perpetual;
you're a fluid in search of its final vial.
The day before your Philadelphia comeback, you cancelled;

10.

ill, the box office said. You had a bruise
on your left calf when you taught a master class
at Merkin Concert Hall—not packed. Risë
Stevens attended, and Albanese. The front rows
were rife with the mad—devoted, malodorous—
Rondine covers waiting to be autographed.
At the reception (I found my way without a pass)
I rustled up to you and dared to grasp
your ring-wild hand and say, "Miss Moffo, I love your last

11.

songs as much as your first. My name is Wayne,
just like your home town. I want to write
your biography." You said, rushed by fame's
demands (the line behind me arched like a tight
"S" a reversed star around a satellite
might madly scribe), "Wayne, I'll keep you in mind."
Crushed, I crossed Columbus against the light
and put my token in the turnstile, the sublime
trapped between my shirt and skin like the whirr of time

12.

turned backwards: restored to my room, to solitude,
I taped the ticket on my journal's alabaster,
and described, in a few words, the altitude
I'd scaled. That torn stub marks our encounter:
time, place, price. There's no trick to a master
class. It's mostly common knowledge: "Sing
each vowel distinctly in 'Non credea'—
convey that you're a bride remembering
a skein you can't untangle without shuddering,"

13.

and other tips on how to impersonate
a stunned girl stumbling toward regeneration—
as I, through clouds, climb to your debut's date.
Do I still love your voice enough to ration
passion into cubits, to risk invasion
of a scarred and sentient star? Anna, in New
York, hello; I don't propose to ruin
your retired, bowered peace with a thousand clues,
this crammed account, through a telescope, of a seven-league view:

14.

peer in the wrong end, and the vision shrinks.
We met eight years before the master class:
in your limo, by the Melody Tent, you wore a mink,
white, and over the rolled-down window's glass
I confessed you were my favorite, and asked
for an autograph. Another fan had lugged
a life-sized poster of your infamous *Thaïs*.
You signed it, and my program, with letters huge,
sweeping, circular, so full they overflowed the page.

III

THE SQUARE OF SWAN

Swan on the shower wall, Steve washes you.
The other grout-joined tiles are useful, pale.
Yours is the only square with a design.
Why am I tempted to address you?

With sponge, and soap dried to the stiffness
of poker chips, Steve makes you clear, exact—
like Poussin's Sabine women, trapped. Then he
plants pansies in our kitchen windowbox

and plays *Manon Lescaut*—to hear side three's
climactic scratch. We're glad the record came
damaged: we love the swallowed unison,
two notes lost in a skip across the grooves.

We rent this apartment for the swan square,
and a sailboat tile on the kitchen floor.
Two tiles: a false foundation for a life.
Steve scrubs the tub; his Pine-Sol leaves no wake.

In the steam room, I face a lanky Jew;
his eyes drill me for oil, his towel askew
as friend slurs into foe, south into north.
Before I steam, I dive in the cold pool

whose colored, blurred, tile arrows indicate
whether my several laps have made a mile.
Chlorine's green alembic sublimes me
into a naiad on Pompeii's mosaic floor. . .

The rift between stability and speed
widens as I stare into the shower's spray,
my swan motionless on its scrubbed wall.
I've said not half enough about the square

itself, predictable form, equal on four sides.
Steve cleans; I cook. How did we first divide
our tasks? Without a treaty, we can trade
terrains, like Germany and Austria,

or pterodactyl and Neanderthal.
I nurse a foolish daydream—that our swan
evolves a friendship with the sailboat tile;
the pansies, trembling in their windowbox

from a rude storm ripping petals and stems,
grow jealous of the swan's and sailboat's bond.
Though tiles can't talk, I hear them whisper
square soliloquies within their separate

sanctuaries. A folding chair, on the porch,
unfolds, as if telling a tale, then stops,
respectful of the somber windowbox
creaking as a gust strikes it, and the swan's moan.

DOCTOR TYPE

lives thirteen floors above and runs a practice
    in the basement. Off-duty he wears jeans
faded so white his butt "reads" (is discernible) across
the street before I recognize
    his face. I cry, "There's Doctor Type!"
in private

jubilation meant for no ear—but he hears.
    Does he understand I mean "archetype"?
I'm not accusing him of being a typist. I type,
and show the symptom of a man
    who types: shiftiness, a Gila
monster's dash

across a rock. I waived wood- and metalshop
    and took two years of typing: invert's choice.
Doctor Type is typical: he foreshadows. He's Jewish
or Arabic, *ça m'est égal.*
    I'm stuck on him. I have a crush.
His plump butt

signifies healing to me: his butt's the part
    from which I guess the Hippocratic whole.
Why don't I see him for a checkup? Premonitions
of embarrassing tumescence:
    Doctor Type's a family man
and would look

askance at the unsocial rising I'm prone
    to suffer when my dark epitome
shifts my testicles between his fingers to test for lumps.
Imagine telling Doctor Type
    the history of my body:
"My flesh, lashed

by desire, couldn't help itself," I'd say,
    an idiot coquette, and Doctor Type
would warn, "Take care what you put in your mouth—make sure it's
        sheathed."
It blinds me to look back that far—
    to the embrace that will have been
the deadly

blow—the way one blast can burst the tympanum.
    My oral temperature's below normal
and I wake up sweating. I have two friends dead, one friend knows
he's dying. These words don't exist
    until I type them, and sometimes
type can't save

a thought from death: it clots, the way my blood
    froze as the messenger drove to the lab—
my blood turned to vermillion icicles, illegible.
I never gave a second tube.
    A spy, I shadow Doctor Type.
He nibbles

halvah between patients, and his practice swells;
    his wife is cooking couscous, Baby squalls.
Who wouldn't envy Doctor Type, or want his love? His butt
makes me wish to be born again—
    I'd be alert this time, sucking
in my gut

to pass more swiftly out. We'd chat—Mom, Doc, me—
    and he would snip my tiny foreskin off.
Bad news blows like a sirocco through my nativity:
"It's not the Promised Land here, kid,"
    warns Doctor Type, and then he drops
the fishnet

in which I squirm. "You are free to go," he says,
    "if you can walk." The receptionist types
my bill, and saves—the cheapskate!—her nearly extinct carbon.
("You never know, there might be bits
    of useful ink left on this sheet.")
Doctor Type

shares the basement with a gay men's gym. My word
    for the hunks who lift weights there is *type:* "Cute
type!" I say when one struts past my window. Types are not drawn
to slight-physiqued non-types like me;
    types only flirt with other types.
My body,

pale, attracts mosquitoes. The bite by my left
    nipple will be worse tonight: I predict
by dawn it will eclipse the swelling on my knee. Wounds shift
powers, degrees, intensities.
    The wound that aches at dusk, by dawn
will be gone.

A PROFESSOR YOUNG AND OLD

My new black horn-rims make me look professorial.
      My father wore such glasses. If the postal
Service were at my disposal, I would Express Mail
      Good dinners to my father every evening.
Meals can influence: if I manage a poached egg
      For breakfast, everything I touch turns to gold,
But if I only find time for cereal, the day
      Follows the curve of an apocalyptic
Documentary. Private proverbs determine me.
      The ritual after-work swim I commit
Fearfully in shallow water opens a trap door
      Onto my middle-class version of vast space:
Five o'clock, when I expect a miracle, a rare
      Journal of a polar explorer, a beer,
A new postage stamp of a shell—"Reticulated
      Helmet"—somehow redeeming my teenage years.
I wore no armor then. I waited for dinner long
      After I should have learned to fix it myself:
On disrupted nights we ate as late as ten-thirty.
      If I postpone voyages until I'm old
I'll die deprived of Rome. But even present places
      Fly by like flimsy newsreels of a tangent
Time. Today's news: Mengele's bones unearthed, New York's
      First high school for homosexuals. I read
These urgent things too quickly, as if I were not fixed
      By what occurs, as cats, cards, and elections
Are fixed. Not one of my large family is serene,
      Or loves life in ways TV shows register.
You have to read our gladness with subtler instruments,
      Scales that pity. We are not a royal flush,
Or even a full house. My newest recreation
      Is relaxing my tense shoulders by my will.
Like cracking knuckles, it passes the time. When I have
      Passed enough time, I will be my father's age,
The age he returns, white-bearded, to forgive Berlin.

RELICS OF THE TRUE CROSS

I escape from my high school charges for one weekend—
    Mattapoisett—and yet their names—Faith, Whitney,
Fiorella—follow me to the shore I christen
    "Sardinia." Puritan Mattapoisett
Becomes free Europe when my groin's in a slingshot strap,
    So why am I thinking of my students' grades?
Visiting my (unnamed) lover's childhood summer house
    Grows easier: now I'm the unquestioned guest,
Short, unsolidly built, preternaturally close "friend"
    Loath to walk barefoot on hot sand. I regret
I didn't sleep with him until late our senior year,
    Too late to meet his grandfather, house-builder
Who left this spot of land. His name, Abramo, I say
    Without expecting an answer. His widow
Makes us *crescenti fritti*—ungreasy as angels
    Fond of dough might wish—and lives far from modern
Names for the carnal sin I commit with her favorite,
    So lets our illicitness rest in her house
And eat for breakfast last night's stale bread in warm chocolate.
    If I were a true fiancée, not ersatz,
I might feel it my privilege to tell the widow
    That though I never knew Abramo, I know
And love his second incarnation: goodness recurs
    When it is that fine. At the end of summer
We'll go to Abramo's first stone house—Boccosuolo,
    A river's mouth too minor for most road maps;
Lifelong marriage is a kind of true cross I collect
    Relics of. My "marriage" seems enviable,
Though secret and *de facto*. Did my parents once think
    That they would love each other in thirty years?
I theorize about the kindness of Italians
    At my own dead Jewish relatives' expense—
Doomed ones I never knew. My great-uncle Abraham
    Is an unstoried blank. In my ignorance
I sometimes think Abramo knows of me and approves.
    The tomatoes his widow grows are sweeter

In their centers than most candy or literature—
    I never knew life to be simple or worth
Rhapsodies until I boiled a chicken for broth
    And saved the meat for salad. "Nunni," they call
The grandmother: generic name, I wish it were mine.
    What does it reveal about my masculine
Disposition that as a young buck I long to have
    This old woman's virtues: growing zucchini,
Folding tortellini for decades of Easter dawns?
    I wax overly psychoanalytic
With my students: this Sunday the beach is overcast
    Because I forced a reticent boy to say
Why the place he wrote about had deep significance.
    Why didn't I leave his early memories
Alone? I'm a sad person and want to see my kids
    Drive through grief and comment on the scenery.
No high school teacher asked me what my name symbolized
    Or guided me to write an essay that gave
The history of a better name. Classmates found
    "Bomb" in my last name and made explosion jokes.
I take Fiorella's errors to Mattapoisett;
    Remembering this little flower's English
Comes from Capri, I pardon unaccustomed spelling
    With a decent grade. Every year it becomes
Clearer I am an introvert who will not better
    Anyone else's lot—even at the beach
Morning fog is my excuse not to converse. My love's
    Name, Steven, I regret is not Stephen, but
He is content with the "v." In the fog, the widow
    Calls "Vain" to me, meaning "Wayne," and I answer.

FAUST IN SEERSUCKER SHORTS

"Do you like opera?" I whispered to him,
    my friend, as *Faust*'s
first notes flooded my heart, and for no reason
    I thought of Barbara

Stanwyck saying the line, "Unquote, I suppose."
    Flamenco music
played backwards in my head. Ten minutes before
    the opera started

we saw *grandes dames* dressed in feathered finery
    formally descend
the stairs as if they were moving toward the eye
    of a private storm,

and he said, "Yes, but not the body stocking
    the devil wears, so
dated, and I can't tell if that's a fig leaf
    or the crotch itself."

The Common Market and its ancillaries,
    like sensible clothes,
begin to vanish. It's Stanwyck who listens
    to Gary Cooper

slowly recite poetry or statistics,
    and when he's finished
she notes that he forgot to end with "unquote."
    They'll get married soon.

I've waited centuries for the dawn to peer
    between the chintz drapes
we bought at Brimfield's antique fair. Flowers in
    clusters make curtains

a love interest, here in bed, where I lie,
  my body lit up
like Faust's. I'm not at home, I'm at the opera
  wearing seersucker.

Polite performance shorts, they stop at the knee
  to reconsider;
cautious Marguerite stops her note in the midst
  of its unfolding.

The usher taps my shoulder, his fingers light
  on the opera's
forehead as a new melody drifts through dust
  and sincerity,

and he says, "You can't sit here, you're Standing Room,
  and this is the Loge."
His flashlight turns its ray on me, and I grow
  allegorical:

this is when the face of nature falls apart,
  and I lose my friend,
or remember that I lost him long before,
  when intermission

chimes summoned us back to our Standing Room perch,
  and I stole, alone,
downstairs to the darker archipelago,
  at what cost you know.

THE MOVING OCCUPATIONS

after seeing Caravaggio's "Bacchus"

Summer light I was driving towards
        Became, up close,
Winter, and at the highway's unexpected
End I shivered and rolled up the windows.
        A minor chord

Swelled in my car's cathedral.
        I love and fear
The moving occupations: your naked
Realistic throat, Bacchus, and your sneer,
        Flushing you from nipple

To the hand that lifts a god's wine glass,
        Cannot intend
To invite, but I follow you into the room
Where I want Paul—nearly a stranger, a foreign
        Man I heard get lost

Traveling through our unresolved
        First conversation
About how Proust lingers on the doorstep
Of sex for hours and never knocks. Motion
        Will not solve

Destination: into the forest—
        Our human, nervous
Days—or into this dream of a clearing, a bed
I love better than any truthfulness?
        Paul's interest

In burning journeys, like a book of prayer
        Put in the pocket
For its weight and not its words, is a cry
I seem to hear out of a deep thicket.
        Our full stare

Falters and goes underground.
    I thought I had
Outgrown wanting to be unsatisfied,
Asking Paul whether the Baroque head
    Weighted down

    With leaves is passionate enough,
        If he sees
What I accept, the invitation of pallor,
The room's goblet spilling, hewn drapery
    Slipping off

    The shoulder—but the boy's enduring
        Eyes are their own
Luxury, with nothing more to say.
In his indifference I am alone, as the car
    Stammers, journeys

    In the difficult direction,
        Turning where the man
Advised not to, following what I know
From boys and fables, not the throats of logicians
    Whose theorems

    Are only beautiful when wrong.
        I used to chase
The pretty girls in third grade to the fence
To marry them; my travels have darkened, Bacchus,
    And the girls are gone.

THE ORNATE AND LOVELY CORNER HOUSE

Oldsmobiles up and down the canals all night:
        how they drive on water
is a mystery beautiful as it is absolute.
        I ask the waiter

the origin of the automobiles riding
        by the fishmonger's,
idling on the water's surface, and he is surprised
        to see me linger

over a question that to him is obvious.
        When I finish my coffee
the night-prowling cars have vanished,
        but from my balcony

tonight, in the ornate and lovely corner
        house, with envy
I will watch the slow procession of the cars
        that are too heavy

to float. And yet they float, a formation
        not reflected
in tomorrow's papers, my generation's
        tone, the tormented

air I am used to hearing in the daily speeches.
        The sublime
visits me so rarely that when it approaches
        there is no time

to regret my lack of preparation
        for its luminous
arrival, its liquid organization.
        This life is formless

and I do not understand most of it:
                    why no children
gather in my cool garden when the heat
                    grows violent.

DOG BITE

I was locking my apartment door, on the way
    To the theater, when I was bitten by a dog,
An ash-gray poodle. Death cannot come on Thursday,
    I thought; I was conscious of my blood, clogged,
Slow-moving; I raised my pants-leg, gray
    Speckled with white, like Formica (this was foreplay

To the revelation) and saw the vampire circlet,
    The open hole the beast's mouth made, my skin
Gashed. The poodle whimpered. It wore a bracelet
    Around its innocent neck. I ate grilled chicken
After the show, and a warm duck salad, and Chiclets
    In the car to heal my breath. I did not sicken

Until the morning. By the time I woke at ten
    A tidal wave had washed my consciousness
Far into the Pacific, past Hawaii, off Japan.
    I called my doctor, who said my recent tetanus
Booster protected me. But I felt as if some hymen
    I didn't know I possessed, powerless

And feminine, had been torn. Harley
    Was the dog's name: after the motorcycle?
I knocked on the owner's door. Was I acting queerly,
    Wishing to speak to her before my blood trickled
To a dead, dry halt? Jo Ann peered out. "I'm fairly
    Ill myself," she said. "Your infection's local

And can't explain your dizziness. No dog
    Bite alone could make you queasy. I'm a dancer,
I'm always dizzy." I called her vet—I wanted dialogue
    With a professional—but there was no answer
In Buffalo, where Harley'd suffered shots in the fog
    Of his dog-consciousness. I called my friend Spencer,

Who worked three years in a rabies research lab.
　　He said, "It's epidemic in New Jersey—five times
The normal incidence." I was imitating Job:
　　Not budging, not complaining, letting God's crimes
Pile up. The bite, no longer raw, had formed a scab:
　　"A scab!" cried Spencer (he looked like Jimmy Sims,

Lead singer in my third grade imitation
　　Monkees rock band). He said, "This is serious.
Why are you being so lax?" I felt the strangulation
　　That facts, paid too much court, impose: gangrenous
Accuracy. But Spencer understands my situation.
　　He is gay, married (as it were), and not promiscuous.

So I followed his advice—I took my bite as law,
　　A voice to be heeded. My mother, too, was bit
By a dog—owned by the Parvus, a family dark as Esau,
　　And lawless. Mrs. Parvu kept their lawn uncut,
And her eldest son had been crippled, speeding at dawn,
　　Drunk, on his motorcycle. He hadn't worn a helmet,

My parents pointed out. Parvu means: already seen?
　　(Or is that *déjà vu*?) Their name has some relation
To vision, the future, or the past. I have been
　　Terrified of the Parvus as of damnation:
Their motorcycles revving up, the boys' hair—duck's-ass, Brylcreemed—
　　And their junky green refrigerator, a vision gleaned

Through their shadeless kitchen window. Mrs. Parvu
　　Told my mother, "That dog doesn't bite.
You must have imagined it." Mrs. Parvu had a tattoo
　　On her left shoulder. Under the weak streetlight
My mother couldn't find the wound, so back to her barbecue
　　Went Mrs. Parvu (an anti-Semite,

We claimed), and my mother called the Health Department,
    Who put the Parvu dog in quarantine.
Thus, it seemed logical to seek my mother's judgment:
    Her words would soothe like powerful Bactine.
She'd survived her dog bite siege, and she is prescient
    About disease: she can read between its lines.

But she didn't answer her phone. Was it negligence?
    Was she out with her new man friend, Jim?
Sympathy, like Mercurochrome, rouged her countenance
    When, as a child, I fell off my Jungle Gym.
Was it more than a mere coincidence
    That my mother and I felt the venom

Of dog spit—dogs lunging at our right calves—
    So close in time, when we'd feared bites for years?
When I reached her, she agreed to call her shrink on my behalf—
    To ask about my bite, not about being queer.
Dr. Fry said, "Just give good wound care." The scarf
    A fifties mother wears when, on the pier,

A sea wind blows, and she wishes to protect her hair—
    A scarf with designs of Paris boulevards:
Well, I wrapped myself around my wound with the care
    That such a woman wraps her scarf, its colors tired,
Around her else-uncovered self. I had a nightmare
    Soon after my mother, walking past the yard

Of the Parvus (a stroll she takes each night
    To lower her blood pressure), heard their dog yap
And felt its teeth, the sharpened, hungry opposites
    Of Sandy's, her childhood dog. My dream: in the gap
Between my mother's life and mine I swam, a floodlight
    Revealing my bad breaststroke and my jockstrap—

I'd left my suit at home. Where's home? In the pool
    Of the emotions that we hold in common—
Our common blood—I dogpaddled. Implausible
    But true, before me yawned the golden canyon
Of Pavarotti's voice—and, moved by each syllable
    He sang, I felt his fine spittle, a poison,

Descend: manna, acid rain. Is my mother's genius
    A venom that makes me foam?
New York is rabies-free, but poison is a Proteus,
    It changes form: the furniture of her home
Is fanged. I am stepping now within the radius
    Of the wet kiss Kurt's mother gave—her dome

Of bouffant hair a kind of synagogue
    To me when I slept over at Kurt's house—
Or the wet kiss, waking me, of Kurt's dog—
    Or the patch of sidewalk I feared, zone of Gladys,
Three houses down, a mutt-haunted faubourg
    ("Gladys"—the name—sounded to me like "lettuce"):

When I braved her porch, my presence set off chimes
    (The chain of red glass squares, a hex that hung
Inhospitably above my head), and her seraphim,
    Five chihuahuas, raced to the screen and sang
A bark version of *Carmina Burana.* I was first stung
    In the company of my mother's delphiniums:

Aloof from my friends, poised on my Sting-Ray's
    Kickstand balanced on our driveway, transfixed
By a game of TV-tag, I felt my bike give way
    And I fell into the flowers. The acoustics
Of the block were acute: my mother, playing hooky
    Across the street, came running, and, allergic

Herself to much of life, she drove me to a specialist
    For shots. I used to bite myself: I paved
The way for Harley. When I got mad, I could resist
    Violence to others by gnawing my own finger. Laved
By my spit, marked by my teeth, I could say—I exist.
    I bite, therefore I am. My finger is still chafed

Where I, for years, have ravaged it—a scratching post,
    A philosopher's stone: animal and human minds
Require a surface to rub against, a host
    For their own incubus. My teeth always find—
As a witch finds her familiar, a widow her ghost
    Husband in Hades—the chewed-on spot, signed

By previous bitings: a place I have not lost.
    I'm glad I never called the Health Department
On Harley: I'm still breathing, and the Boy Scouts
    Taught me to live in fear of those omniscient
Beasts that know the art of reading human thoughts
    Through the ill-concealing walls of an apartment.

A goldfish tossed in a garbage can—a good
    Fish-friend for a week—haunts me as if it were a poet.
My second pet, a turtle, died of dryness. It was my étude
    In life, and I botched the exercise. I forgot
To dispense its daily tablespoon of food,
    And the water grew green and still with thick brine clots.

My sister, in puberty, picked up a stray,
    Without my mother's consent, and named it "Tish."
We kept it in the garage, and got it spayed.
    I always felt poignant when I gazed at its dish
Of mess, but I would turn from pity, go in to play
    My Bach. That dog bite week, my plants perished

From the heat, and I wore shorts, without a bandaid
  To cover the wound. That way, when people asked
To see the bite, I could blazon it, like a newlywed
  Proud of her ring. My bite, after all, is an odalisque—
Nude, reclining, aloof, and staring straight ahead
  Into the future, like a fitted death mask:

When I even think about the bite, I get an ache
  Above my stomach, as if I can't digest
The memory of the dog, wandering in the wake
  Of a carnival down a dusty road, on an overcast
Thursday in the Veneto (I think of Proust's Balbec,
  The sea-town where he longs for girls, for the conquest

Of time): we asked, in a town whose name I can't recall,
  For directions to the *cimitero*—a cemetery
Celebrated for the tomb of the Brionvega family.
  (We didn't know this yet, but our friend Bill
Had died that week of AIDS.) No one in the carnival
  Procession understood our question. A collie—

I am guessing, I have never cared to know the names
  Of the various dogs—trailed behind the cars
And carts and bicycles, and having searched in vain,
  We thought, for the cemetery—was it hidden in that far
Mass of trees?—we took our eyes from the road, and cries of pain
  Two seconds in the future almost struck our ears

With what we had not done, but nearly done:
  The dog—collie? Saint Bernard?—limped offstage,
Old and gray. We'd almost hit it. A woman in cretonne
  Shook her finger at us in a feint of rage.
Was it her dog? Then we found our Brionvega tomb,
  And signed the guest book, and visited the graves.

THE ANSWER IS IN THE GARDEN

I wanted proof of God's hunger, but no sacrifice
    Had tempted Him to eat for a thousand years.
I laid a kleenex on my windowsill for altar
    And offered the Sweet Tarts that I'd shoplifted.
Waking to find my candy there and slightly dusty,
    I struck back by wasting the Sabbath in bed
Blindly stumbling through *Nietzsche and Christianity:*
    Its language was impossible, but I wished
My parents to know that I'd been abused by the powers.
    I don't mean this to be a dull history
Of my reading life, but what I'm drawn to say begins
    With a book that, like a trick of light, opened
The subject of death which I have not the power to close—
    I must begin with *The Supernatural*'s
Infrared pictures of London witch covens dancing,
    Nude men and women with cellulite bellies
That looked pregnant—for a man is said to be pregnant
    When he sees the future like a charcoal sketch
Rising from the undrawn. The book showed dimes on shut eyes
    Of possessed Caribbeans, and a dead boy
Knocking on a door for centuries—the runaway
    I dreamed peered into my room because he was
Exiled by his Lancastrian parents and had need
    Of delinquent's shelter. Would I let him break
My window open? I'd read about his court ordeal
    In a Scholastic magazine, a special
Issue about the other world: the story promised
    A sequel that never came, and the years passed
With the boy stationed eternally outside my room
    Inquiring if I were generous enough
To offer my floor to his thorn-scarred back. A lost boy
    Whom circumstance has reduced to trespassing,
With soot face he implores me through the window, and knows
    That after supper, when trees howl, there will be
Time for us to conspire. I can't dismiss such stories.
    In Michigan, a haunting light never left

A lakeside mansion: the red glow behind the rosebush
    Watched the daughter study her geography
And the chandelier fell on the dining room table
    Just as lights had crashed one century ago
On the late master's head. *De rigueur* campfire fables—
    Bermuda Triangles, Kennedy death plots—
Touched me as only the watery, unrigorous
    Mind can be shaken: of my epiphanies
I demand little more than an impression of speed,
    Illusion that I am moving toward an end
Unseen by all but the wisest spectators, who ask
    Not for real prophecy, but the skeleton
Of enchantment, private auguries, a ringing phone.

    Omens come in series. Their recitation
Takes its toll, my legs feel weak. At the airport we saw
    A lean man—attractive, consumptive, or just
Swindled by experience—smoking at a pay phone.
    Facetiously, I named him "Death in Venice":
I'd read Mann as tourist's homework. Our pre-boarding hours
    He spent passionately on the phone—to whom?
When a second phone at our gate rang, he stared at me
    As if I knew, within my sealed universe
Of coincidence, who was calling. The central fact,
    Simple, but difficult to put into words,
Was the note addressed to my traveling companion,
    Stefano Marchetti, on August 30th,
In Venice—a note waiting for him at our hotel
    When we arrived—and we immediately
Questioned how the correspondent knew to send the note
    Here to the Locanda Sturion, because
No friend of ours had this address, and this was no friend,
    But a stranger, Carlo, who'd misaddressed
His note: he'd written to a *Silvano* Marchetti,
    Not to my Stefano. A coincidence?
Carlo called to repeat his plea that in an extreme
    Moment he needed shelter from great danger—
Would we permit him to spend the night on our bare floor?
    I felt this was the last crisis of a life

That had for years been drawing near to some precipice
    In secrecy and quiet, and now must claim
The loyalty of friends. Carlo could not understand
    That Stefano was not Silvano, that we
Knew nothing of their turbulent history, of errors
    Committed between them in the confusion
Of a foreign country. Stefano forbade Carlo
    A place by our side, but nothing explained how
Mysteriously Carlo had discovered the spot
    Where an approximation to his lost friend—
Nearly the same person, but a skewed portrait, misplaced
    Or damaged by rain—was passing through Venice
The night of the other's distress. I was visited
    By dreams of a weeping, faceless Silvano
Sought by Carlo through the universe; "Silvano" seemed
    A gap in the perfect world where a spirit
Heard the command to return to dust and disobeyed,
    Lingering a few minutes longer on earth
To ask of us, the living, a difficult favor—
    To hide him in our room, where his pursuer
Might neglect to look. If he could weather out the night
    He would tell us in the morning the answer
That blazed in that second when he heard his time was up.
    In the morning, a bald man with one black glove
Passed me in a square, and the next day, in Vicenza,
    He reappeared, Tarot-like, at our hotel
Where within the long arcade up Monte Berico
    I saw him stop to remove the glove and show
One false hand, like white chocolate, or soap. I've neglected
    To mention the most impressive augury—
Also the most conventional: in Venice we saw
    A coffin lowered into a gondola,
Mourners oared with the dead body down the dark canal—
    The ultimate in picturesque, similar
To my foolish humming of the Hoffmann "Barcarolle"
    As we strolled by Rio dei Mendicanti . . .

In New York, a letter marked "hand-delivered" is taped
    To our door: Stefano's friend, Metro, has died—

His lingering cold which no one took seriously
    Wrapped him in a coma. Now he is ashes
Scattered in his backyard garden, planted just last spring.
    Metro died on the thirtieth of August,
The night we arrived in the city of gondolas,
    The night we received the enigmatic note
To Silvano: man telephoning in the airport,
    The one black glove, name I could call my terror.
Did Metro's soul, done with the body, come to Venice
    In the extreme moment? I've never written
An elegy: none of our small circle had yet died.
    This is not musical enough to sing his
Soul down the river mine and yours must, too, go down, but
    Metro needs a mourning song, not the white mask
We bought for him in Venice. We visited Keats' grave:
    The whole of Rome seemed to radiate around
Untimely death, a fact seen through a distractingly
    Beautiful circuit of tears. When I am dead
I may be wise enough to say it well. On the plane
    Back to New York I dreamed that Italian
Church facades also existed in America,
    But in our country they were not memorable:
I saw the intensity of a better epoch
    Drained from the columns—I could almost hold on
To pieces of the old distinction before I saw
    It fade into air. In San Gimignano
I felt a presentiment that I would spend next year
    Sanctifying my dreary premises: in court
My parents battle on my twenty-seventh birthday.
    I'm glad to age, greedy for each year I add
To my abacus, irrespective of sunderings
    That mar the date. Metro died at thirty-five,
A waste huge enough that I can address my parents
    Within the magic circle of his passing:
Let the fact of my body be the *Piramide*
    Memorial to your once marriage, and don't
Cry about things only seventy-five-percent sad—
    Save tears for the fully tragic. Metro's last
Fevered sentence was, "The answer is in the garden."
    I meet Metro in his still-tended garden

And I am wearing his clothes, given to me because
   We are one size. I want to read Metro's lips
For he is facing the invisible, and speaking
   Eloquently of efforts taken too late,
The many souls wandering in the air, not pinioned
   As children are. I am too corporeal
To hold the attention of one so weightless, to say,
   In a tone of sad confusion, that the good
Suit he wore in life fits me well, too well, like a charm.